Avarice & Ice

Poetic Longings

Jamie L. Jewels

BookLeaf
Publishing
India | USA | UK

Made with ❤ on the BookLeaf Publishing Platform

www.bookleafpub.in

www.bookleafpub.com

Dedication

*For the things inside all of us
that we never fully nurtured.*

Preface

Avarice & Ice began as an idea for a poem, then became said poem, and over time grew (much like greed itself) into this poetry book you're now about to read. It delves into the mind of a young woman trying to figure out her place in this world and where all the messy feelings of life fit into that space. We, as humans, cannot help but to want more of everything: From the simplest of things, to reliving old memories, wanting to better ourselves, and hoping that the paths we walk are right.
This is to all the weird ones.

May your journey be a prosperous one.

Acknowledgements

I would like to thank the one person that has always had my best interest at the forefront of their mind, my husband, Robert J. Yielding. Thank you for putting me first every time. Make sure that you put yourself first sometimes too.

Save Me

Save me a summer.
A place that is warm.
Days of cold hang ahead
That breed only scorn.

Save me a seat.
A place right beside you.
I want us to watch the Perseids
As they shoot into view.

Save me some time
To walk among the flowers.
Let's roll about the grass
And talk for hours.

Save me from my loneliness.
I haven't spoken in a while.
Save me, at least, one more summer
To ease this winter of exile.

Save me, save me,
Please, if you can.
Only warmth can melt
The hearts of man.

Icarust

I broke you
Because I was angry.
You stayed out of the way.
Beautiful.
Serene.
A porcelain angel holding flowers.
Hit through the stomach
With a metal Tervis cup.
Glass everywhere.
Shattered.
I broke your wings.
Nothing a little glue can't fix.
If you ever try to fly,
Forget it,
You will only die.
Wings melting in the light
Just like Icarus.
A cold lump of feathers and marble flesh.
Piecing you back together.
It wasn't your fault.

Now we're both a mess.
I'll hold you together
Until the adhesive dries.
Some places too chipped.
Certain pieces unfound.
Maybe they will not notice.
Maybe you'll enjoy more time
On the ground.
Hidden back in the corner
Where they won't see you too close.
Where your cracks become cracks
In the floor, near the dirt.
No one will inspect you,
Of this I am sure,
Because angels are never prayed to
In this house made of hurt.

Blossom

Miss Dickinson died for beauty
Too well adjusted to her room.
Delicately rooted as a flower
Scarcely though.
For is a flower named a flower
If it never lives full bloom?
A life lived on in letters.
The keeper of one's key.
No one can judge, or pressure,
The things they finally read.
When you've lived in peace,
And left them
A handful of some seeds,
A fool will toss and never plant them
Only seeing an ugly, tiny thing.
It never matters what we breed.
A bloom is not a blossom.
A flower not a seed.
Woman not woe.
Alone not lonely.

These may or may not be.
But a seed will surely stay a seed
If that's all you ever see.

Hipster

I am just gonna say it,
I liked you first.
I read your pages.
I ate your words.

When you moved
I watched in awe.
When you beckoned
For an ear
I came at your call.
I held you dear.

You made me
Feel something new.
Feel alive
For creation.
I finally desired
Something grand.

You made me

Chase away blue
Tears that always swelled.
I picked out
The best parts of me.
I held them out in my hands.

I wanted everyone to drink
The fluidity of your charms.
I sought to share
Because good things
Are better when you can talk
To someone who understands.

I did not know that silence
Was bliss
And the ignorance of this
Is what forms fools.
I loved you first.
You know I did.

So, how come now
It feels like I never did.
Because no one heard me
When I rejoiced your name,
Quoted your words,
Or drew your many curves.
They forgot.

They didn't listen.
Was I on mute?
Did someone far away
Read my lips
And write this down?

Write out graphs,
Create charts,
All pointing to your rise?
To your birthing star?
Now they don't realize
How hard it all was
To think we were so close.
My friend when I was alone,
When I was lonely,
When I was no one.

Now I'm just one,
Of many,
To follow your page.
To take you home.
To fall asleep in a daze
And wake to another meme.

This must be a scheme.
A sham.
A front.

A trend.
And I'm offended.
I can't defend,
What cannot be protected,
What has no need.

This seed,
Of hearts,
Of likes,
And shares...
It's overwhelming.
I cannot take the stares
From around this world
As they squeeze you dry
Of all you've done.
They breed and feed
Like endless animals.

No consequences.
No, only fun,
Only new,
Only things that unmake you,
You.

I liked you first.
I will admit.
And it stings

When they say I never did.
It was all because of the internet.
A fantasy caught in a net
That I want to free
Of society.
For it to be safe.
Unseen,
Again, only for me.
I am sorry.
I can't give you fame.
But you and I are not the same.
I just want to laugh, and love,
And be amazed once more,

Not because of them,
But because of you.
I was here first.
I am here too.
People can be the worst.
I am saying that I like you.
I always will.
Know, when the trends end,
I will be here still.

Avarice & Ice

Avarice and ice
Make excellent company.

One is ambitious,
One rather cold,

But there are no distinctions.
Saying such would be too bold.

Some say riches make you evil.
Some say they freeze your soul.

I say money is convenient
And, with that, I gladly sow.

The roots of my afflictions.
The head that, now, I hold.

Those somber cataclysms
Of war within my bones.

Thirsty

I'm tired of telling you what happened
When you blackened out your mind.
I hate seeing how much the hurt
Makes you wish to erase time.
You say that you're too small
But, when you go weightless,
Nothing feels more heavy.
Your pains no longer hide.
What is it that ails you?
The shackles kept inside.
You wrap them up so neatly.
No wonder they ask, "Why?"
Why do we feel lonely
When the masses gather by?
Why do we think nothing
Is better than pastimes?

I hate telling you what happened
When you dive in way too deep.
I'm tired of seeing eyes that bow

Down to the secrets that we keep.
You say that you're okay.
That you didn't drink too much.
But how come you look so sad
When the news does, surely, come?
I know what ails you.
Something real inside.
You wrap it up in ribbons,
But you can't muffle out its cries.
I know that you feel lonely
When no one understands.
I know that you think it's hopeless
But, I'm here, helping you stand.
I want you to remember
All the ones that got you home.
I want you to remember
How much love you can lean on.
I want you to remember
That it's okay to cry.
I want you to remember
You don't have to hide your eyes.

But what happened
Is just a story
You heard
Nothing
Very

Real.
So, I tell you
What transpired,
Hoping,
That I won't have to,
One day,
Still.

What It Was

I don't usually feel like talking,
But when I do,
I always say something wrong to you.
If only I could censor the crevices of my mind,

To ease their chaotic plight,
To give my thoughts more time.
But I am only human.
What did you expect?

I don't have a plan.
You see, my mind's a wreck.
Why is it that my limbs go to sleep so fast?
And yet, my brain cannot get past,

The memories that tie me down,
And tighten up my forlorn frown?
The things that beat their way into me,
Bruise me daily,

As per their creed.
And yet I'm something
Besides this husk;
A soul that has a purpose, I know it must.

In the depths inside, a whisper stirs,
A flicker of hope, a yearning that recurs.
Despite the chaos, the doubts, the pain,
A realization dawns, a truth to gain.

I am more than the sum of my flaws,
More than the mistakes that leave me in awe.
A spirit bound by human frailty,
Yet in yearning for more I selfishly plea.

In the stillness of the night, I hear it clear,
The gentle voice that dispels fear.
I am a vessel for something grand,
A thing with a purpose, a force to command.

So, I journey forth, through the darkness deep,
Embracing the scars, the secrets I keep.
For in the depths of my being, a light does glow,
Guiding me forward, as I continue to grow.

And yet, I know what I know
Is still not enough.

These reaper seeds sow
Out words making me tough.

My body may sleep,
But my mind stays awake.
As the words overflow,
I desperately shake,

Out all the constipated
Feelings for you.
Realizing I must have been
Something forgotten once too.

Frozen In Place

You say nothing.
A welcomed ghost.
Forlorn figure.
Mother of jealousy.
If I act cold
It's because I care.
An ice queen
Shielding a heart of flame.
We avoid our eyes.
A mutual, apathetic, glare.
Moving with regality.
Moving any-way, freely, in this game.
Icey palms
Hoping to form warm pairs.
I want to melt
But this power ensnares.
I'm to blame.
I said what I felt.
Am I the only one that cares?
How can everything change and stay the same?

Frozen in place.

Just A Game

Life and Death
Are in a game,
To steal your heart,
To take your name.

They roll on dice.
They deal out cards.
They hope to win
Against all odds.

Tis nothing new.
It's how they play.
A forfeit here.
Another gain.

We can't compete.
Their hands are locked.
We only move
As we are taught.

Pawns for them;
Their Kings and Queens.
A life long-lived is a win,
Or so it seems.

Death doesn't mind.
He's seen all things.
And Life creates
As it keeps losing,

More and more pieces,
As Death keeps choosing.
It's frustrating
But we must let them play.

For at the end,
Both sides get their way.
They pause momentarily.
They end in draws.

No victory complete.
Life and Death are in this game.
That never ceases,
Yet always claims.

Letting Go

What do I do?
Your mistakes
Are yours
Not mine.

I'd take them
As my own,
But it'd be an un-welcomed
Home.

You're not alone.
We're all stained.

Strained.

Trying to hold onto
The things we no longer need
But think we will miss.

Only Feelings Remain

Scarfs of rich red
Tied around our throats.
Hoping to ease us
Only causing us to choke.

Stumbling into rooms,
Not our own,
Wondering where we've gone.
Placid strolls through egg-shell tombs.

When they ask, "What was said?"
I won't be able to answer.
I can only tell you
That I feel awful.

My memory is a sham,
But the feeling remains.
I can no longer see the face,
But the imprint of oil on the glass
Stays the same.

I don't want to make you feel this way.
So, I say nothing.
Knowing the things it won't change.

You gave me this noose,
I wear casually,
Against my skin.

Hoping you can, one day, understand
How tightly you've wrapped me up.

Hoping you can stand,
To walk alongside me,
Since we share a shade of red.
Maybe, if we walk steadily,
We won't get hung-up
On what was said back then.

Please Change The Topic

I don't like writing about love,
Because what's the point
If it's already lost?

Some aches never fade.
Didn't we speak just yesterday?
Holding out my arms
Makes me feel ashamed.

They say a love lost
Is a friend gained.
But that's not the case
If one, is both,
It's all the same.

When was the last time
We talked or kissed?
Memories get moldy
With every day that's passed.

I no longer write for you.
Seventeen-year-old fever dreams.
I cannot be stingy.
I write for me.

Probably some un-addressed insecurities.

Looking back does nothing
But turn you into a pillar of salt.
Tears stained on pillowcases.

In case you forgot,
I gave you all I had.
The emptiness I had to fill;
I feel it still.

If I write it down
It makes it real.
The things left between us,
I fear,

They might never disappear.

Of Fleas & Filth

You're surprised I act the way I do.
Why I choose myself over any of you.
Once, I tried to share some wealth,
But forgot that I was born of fleas and filth.

You took, boasted, then took some more.
You scoff to think I'm wise,
Having asked, "What did you come here for?"

Now, I sit here on this stained, carpeted, floor.
Thinking, "If only I could've done, for them, more."

Being from filth you get used to fleas.
Welcoming them in.
Dismissing their disease.
How foolish to think you could reach the top.
Even if I could have,
Would I have found what I had sought?

I lay inside a house that is not my own.

Wondering where it all went wrong.
Picking fleas off my legs,
I dissociate into a daze.
You're surprised I act the way I do.
Don't you know?
I was taught the ways of filth
From you.

Greed

Mr. Frost thought the world might end in fire,
Or that it might end in ice.

From what I've witnessed of man's ire
I say the world's demise is neither.

The end of times will come through greed.
With bulging eyes and twisted deeds.

Hands that only know to take.
Heads that turn from human's sake.

I think I know enough of malice
To say that this destruction's planned.

Petty schemes that breed more gallus
Leave man with no room to stand.

Floriography

No one ever talks of flowers.
They never want to feel the rain.
They anticipate the death of weeds;
Of things that hide other things.

No one notices the infinity of grass.
They never want to see the flowers drop.
They anticipate the perennials' bloom.
They wish they always had more room.

No one ever talks of flowers.
They never want to admit they die.
They anticipate the rain to come
To ease the bloated clouds above their minds.

No one cares to think of weeds.
They never want to give way to be gobbled up.
They anticipate they will always get cut down
Because things always hide in other things.

Pink Noise

I want to sleep inside the rain;
For it to pass through my mind.
Though I hear it, beating on the rooftop,
I want to feel just fine.

I want to roll in satin sheets,
As the thunder swelters by.
I want to roll with steady quakes.
I want to sleep this time.

I want to dream of pretty fae;
For them to help me fly.
Though I know it is not real,
I want to feel alive.

I want to roll about my bed,
As the thunder bids goodbye.
I want to dream of pure pink noise.
I want to sleep this time.

Focus

Take your picture.
Focus.
I don't need to be noticed.
I just want a little notice
Before you throw me out.

It's a mess,
Taking photos of me.
Can you take this from me?
I'm full.
What do you make of me?
Wait, what, sorry I drooled.
God dumped some cherries
In my pits.
Gotta scoop them out.
Can you handle it?

Go, go, now can you
Focus?
Better sit still.

Don't you blow this.
Feeling like a flimsy birthday candle,
Cake over wishes,
Another thing taken for granted.
Throw me out.
Take me away.
A heart made of wax.
Hands formed from clay.
And you say it's good,
That I look great,

But if you printed me out
Would you frame me today?
Would you want to display
The things that you took?
The things zoomed in on.
Trade one look for a look.
You instead hide me.
A burden no gift.
You shove me in a nook.
It's not your aesthetic.
There's no place for me here.

I want to be closer.
Press my hands to a mirror,
You flash me a smile,
As the light bursts, sure enough,

I thought I was ready.
Let's forget it.
It's done.

Not What I Wanted

This isn't how I wanted things to go,
Surely, this, you must also know.
The path we tread feels lost and worn,
The promises we made, now also torn.

In the hallowed silence of the night,
I grapple with the fading light.
The dreams we shared, now cast astray,
In the shadows of yesterday.

I thought we'd walk hand in hand,
Through the trials of life, and always stand.
But fate had other plans in store,
Leaving us broken, wanting more.

The echoes of our laughter fade,
In the quiet moments, memories cascade.
The love we nurtured now withers and dies,
As we uncover the truth behind the lies.

In the ruins of what we once held dear,
I search for solace, for words of cheer.
But the wounds run deep, the scars remain,
A poignant reminder of a love in vain.

So, I stand alone, in the aftermath,
Haunted by ghosts of our war-torn paths.
This isn't how I wanted things to go,
Surely, this, you must also know.

Passing By

Are your skies still, somehow, blue
Beneath grey clouds that obscure you

Is the light that you demand
Something, to you, I can lend

Does the rustle in the leaves,
That frolic when the tree limbs weave,
Bring about to you some ease

Is there, then, something underneath
Some valiant nature to bequeath

What secrets, tell me, do you keep
What pains cast spells that make you weep

Is there something, anything, that I can do
To break this curse that defines you

I feel great weakness in this way

To greet your pleas with more delay

To have the darkness passing by
Fleeting glances, clouded, eyes

And still to see those shades of blue
Those, light-filled, patches that emit from you

Bring with them hope
This much is true

Harder Than I Thought

It feels colder,
Than it should, here.
Memories are now bolder
Then they, once, appeared.

Is it because I still drive past you every day?
Unable to see you
Any differently.

I
Feel
Stuck
Between
Two
Hard
Places.

Though, even if you were rubble,
I couldn't see you
Any other way.

Day
By
Day
By
Day

It feels warmer,
Than it should, here.
Memories are now colder
Then they, once, appeared.

Specter

A specter lifting clouds.
Rising with the night.
The days blur by in shrouds.
Have I any fight?

Have I any doubt
That the moon will, once more, rise?
Yes, the sun ascends devout.
I, myself, am more unwise.

I, myself, am more a ghost
Passing through this land.
Searching for a welcomed host.
Grasping for a hand.

Grasping for a way
Like a specter blowing wind.
I want to live this day!
But, alas, all things must end.